Anim...
Stretc...

Written by **Marcia Vaughan**
Illustrated by **David Febland**

ScottForesman
A Division of HarperCollins*Publishers*

2b

I can be a bird.

2

I can be a cat.

I can be a camel.

I can be a frog.

I can be a snake.

I can be a fish.

Animal stretches keep us fit!